Coloring book belong to

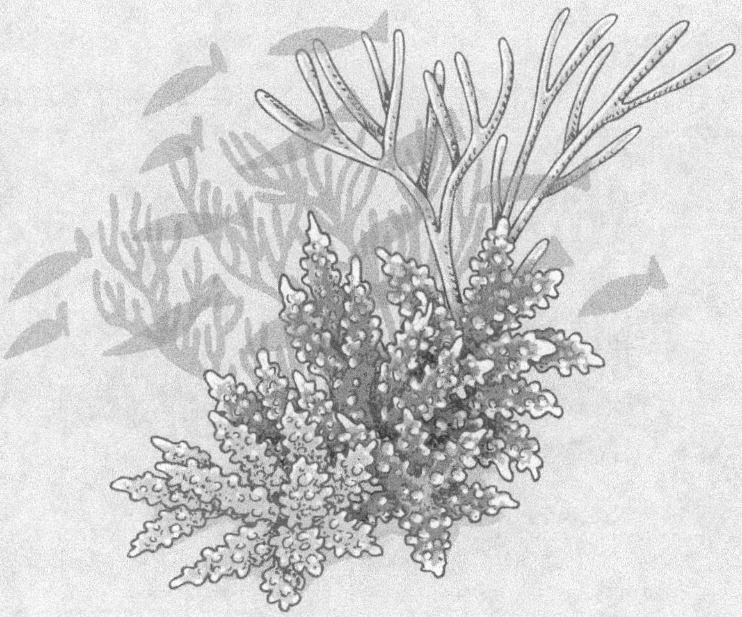

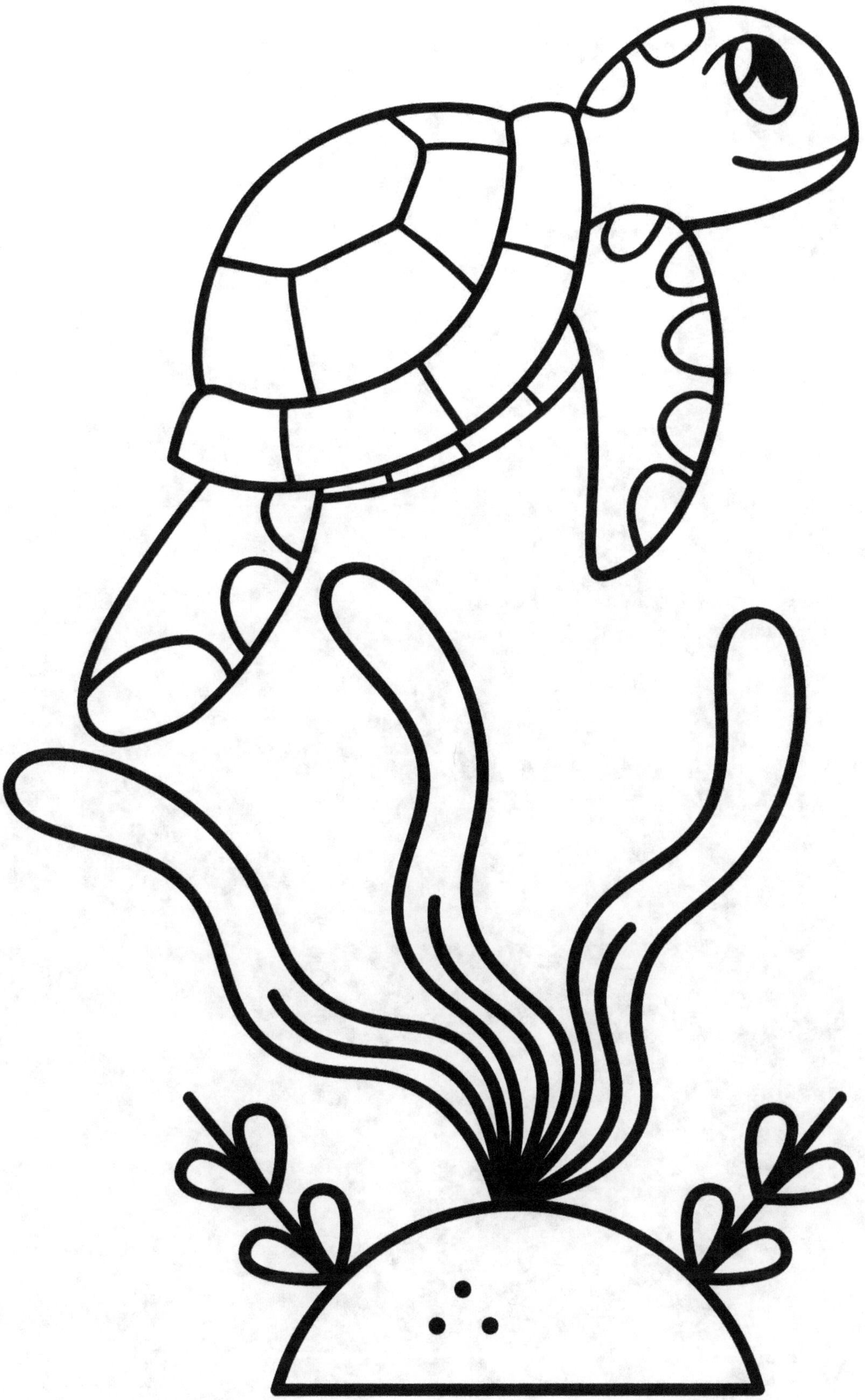

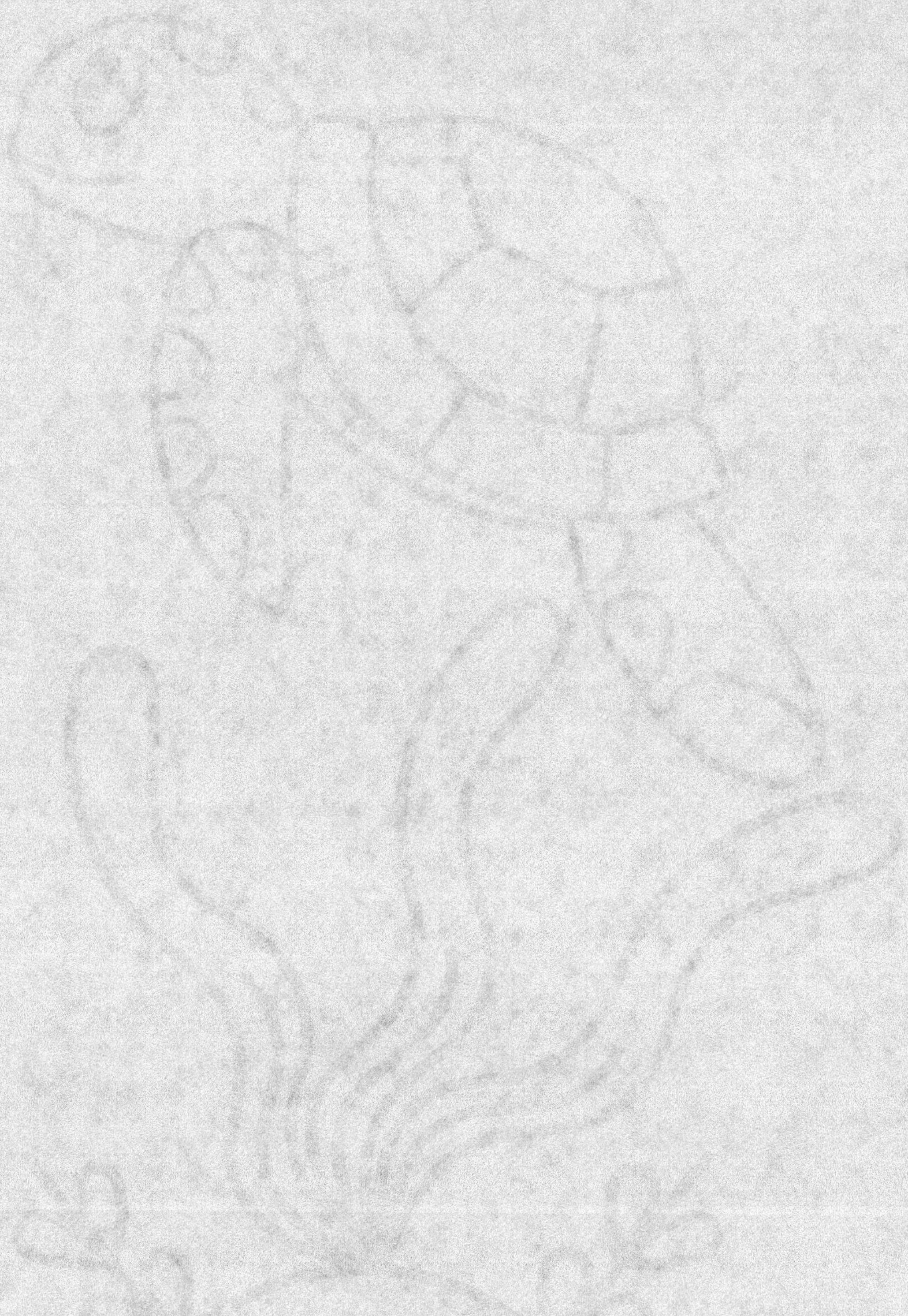

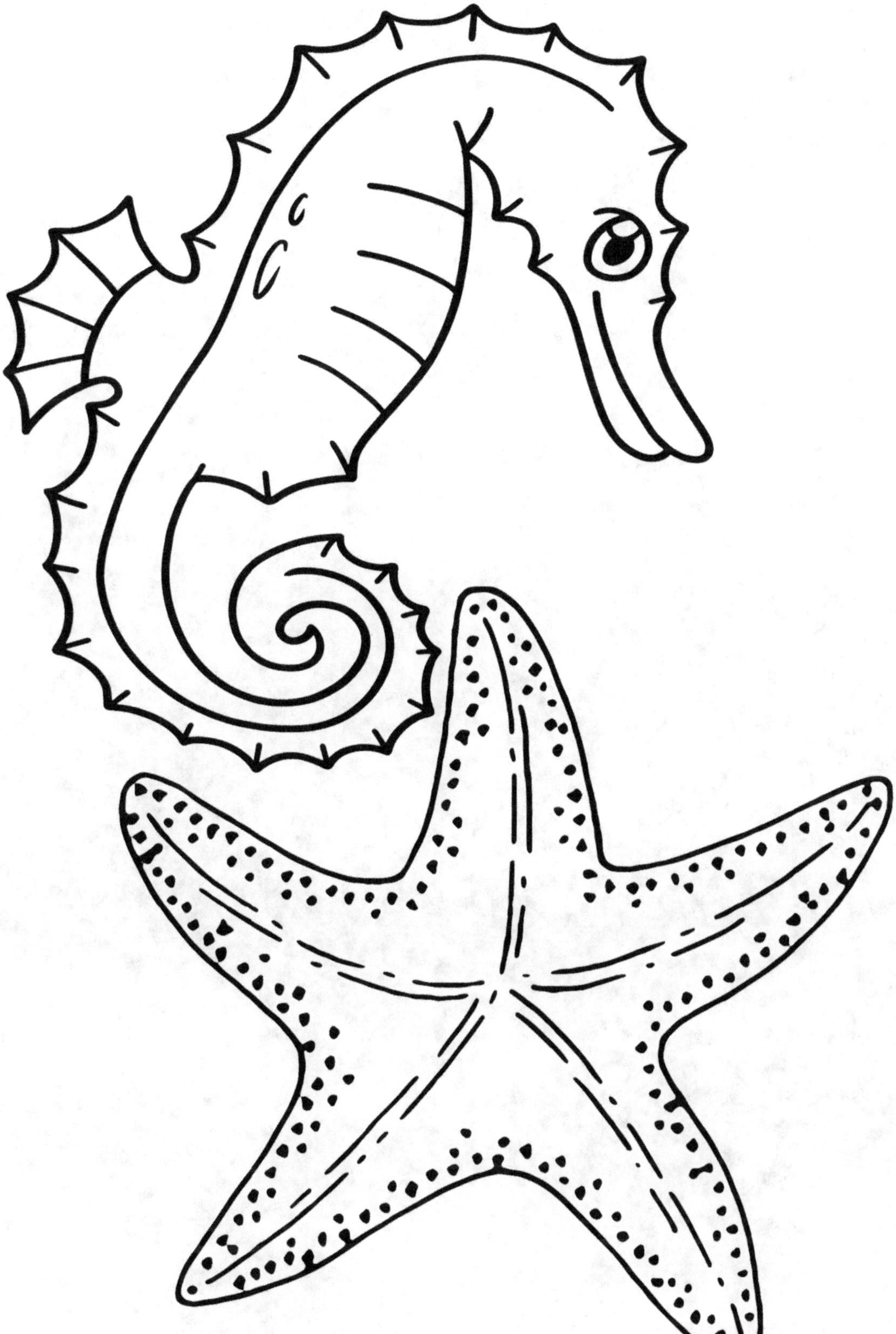

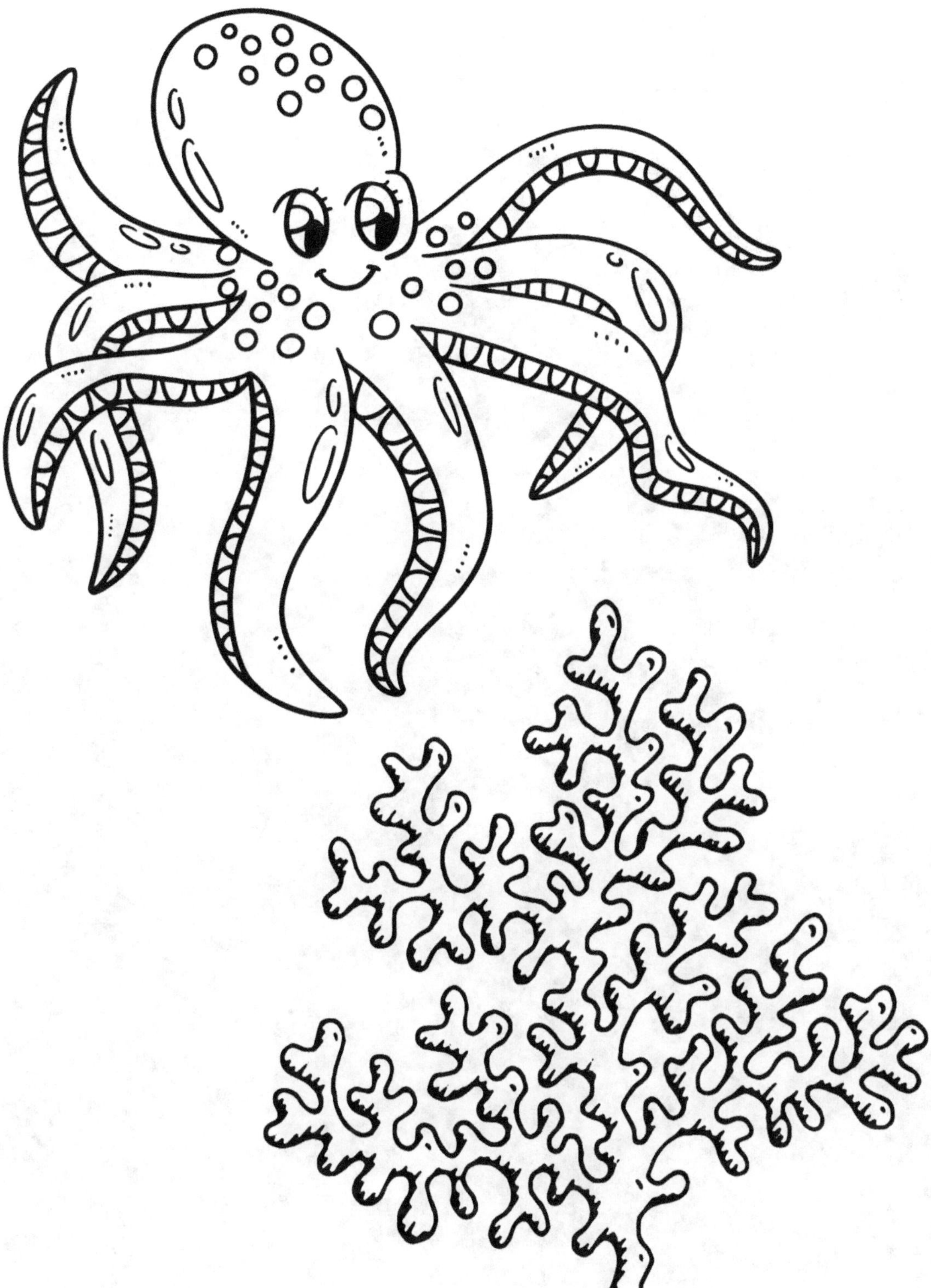

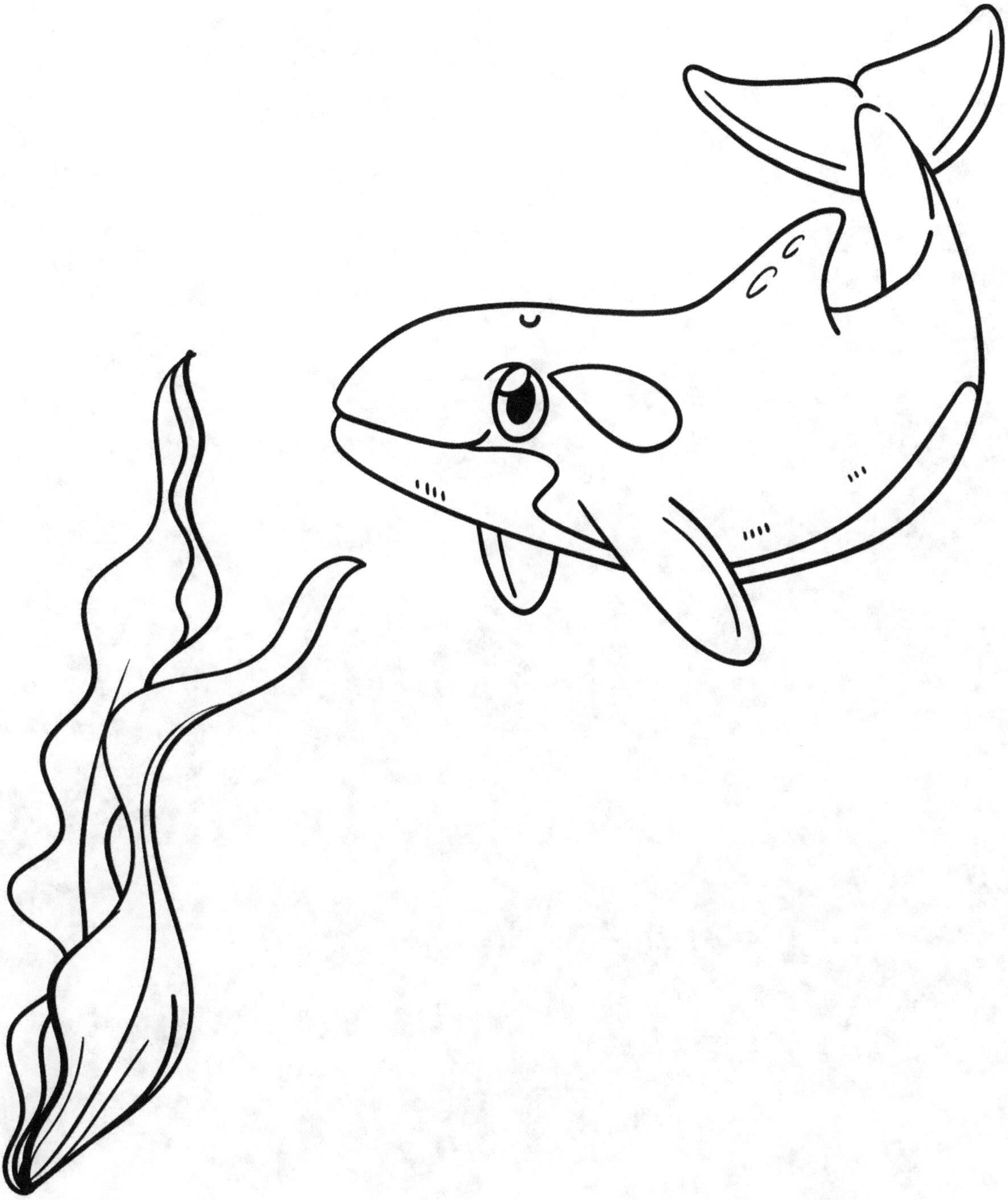

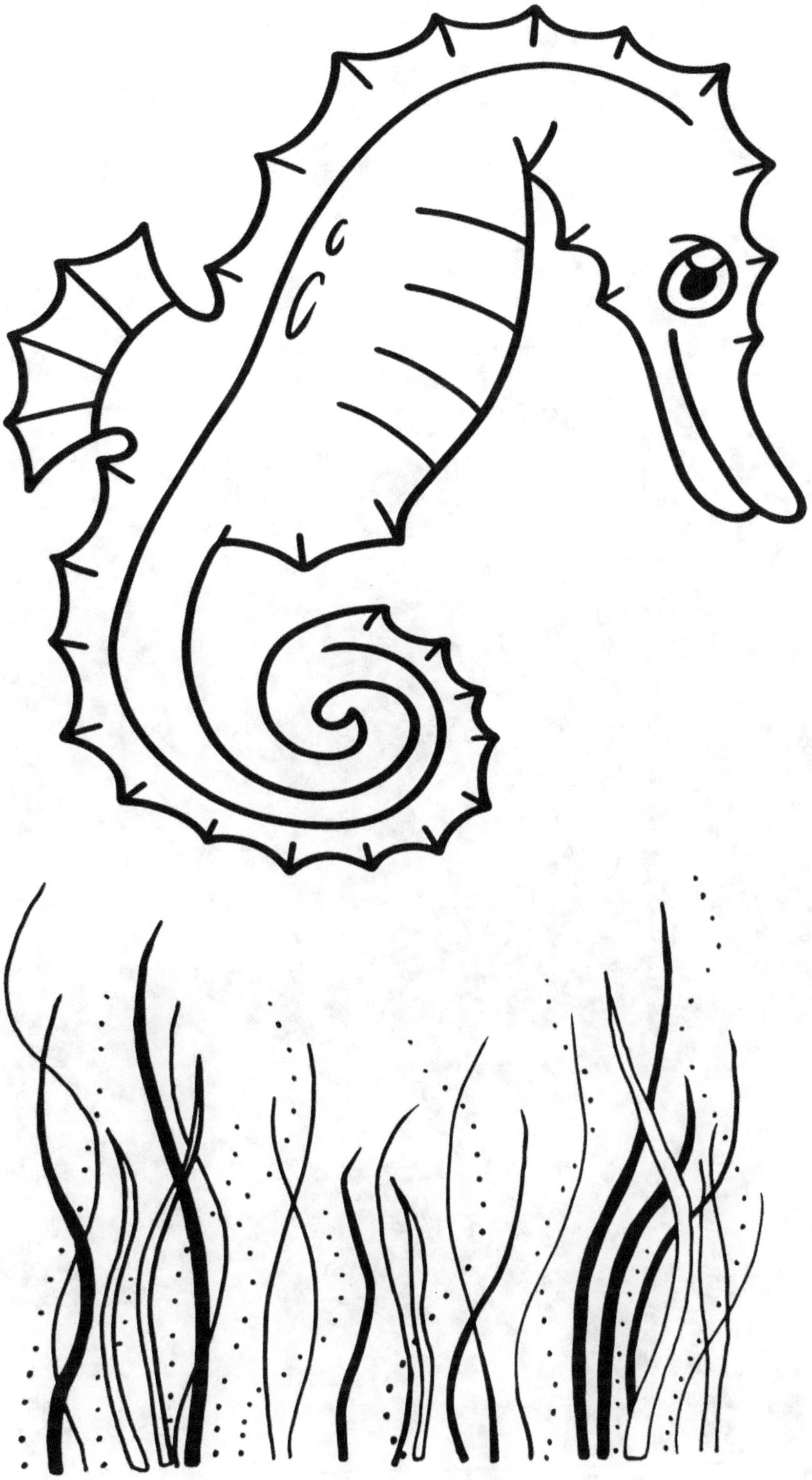

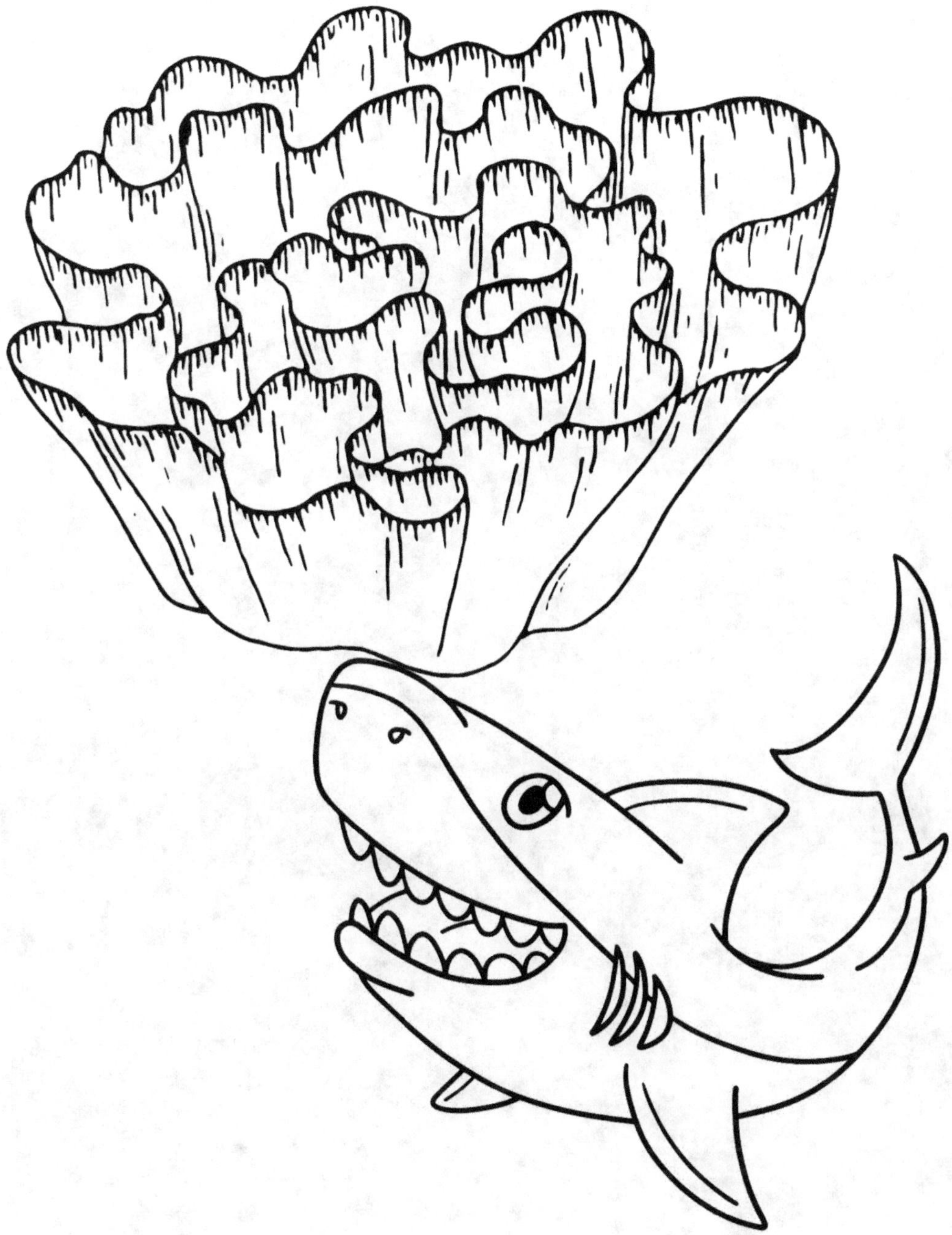

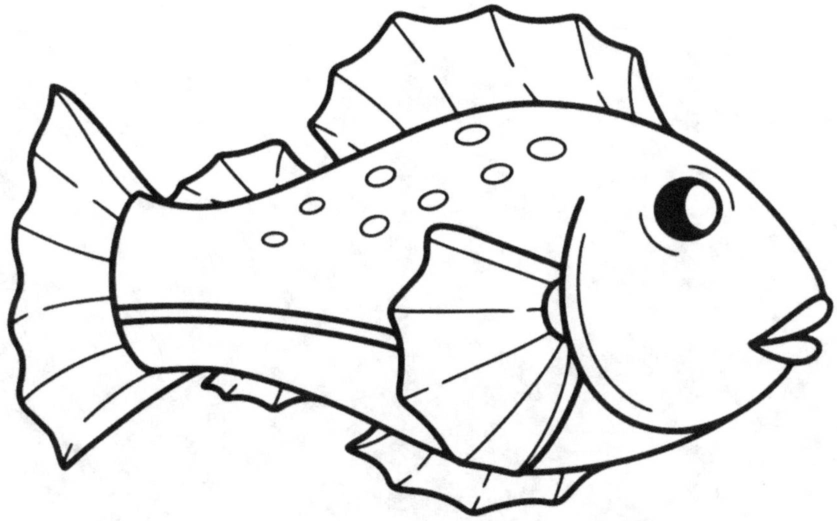

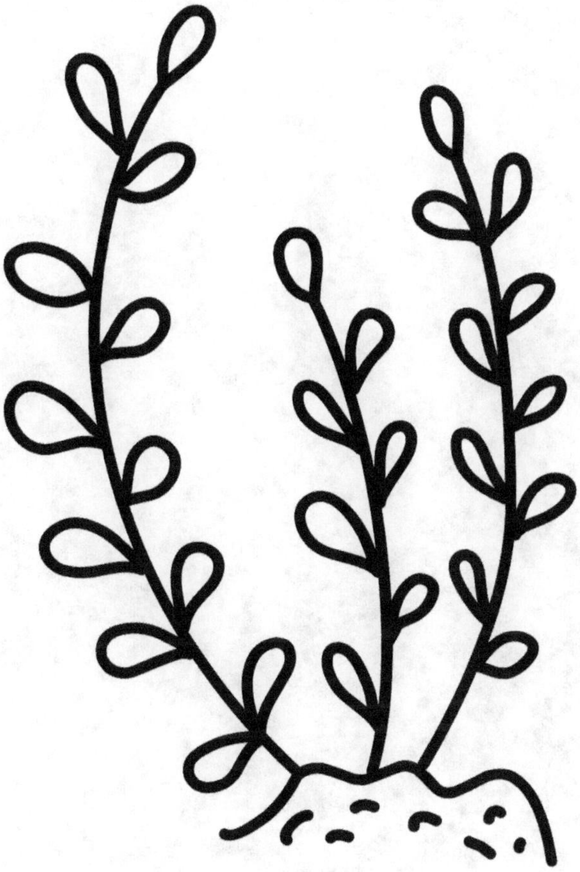

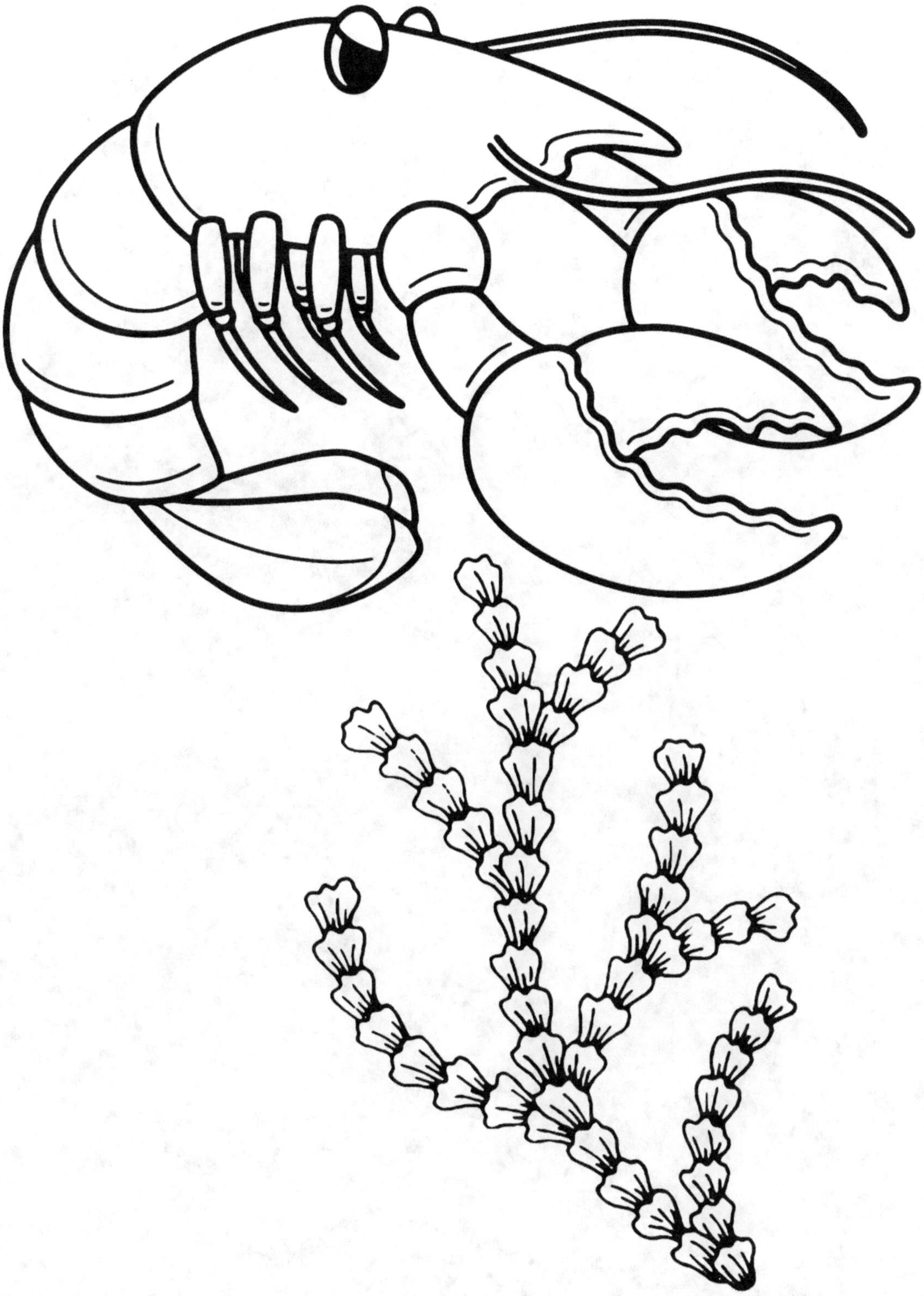

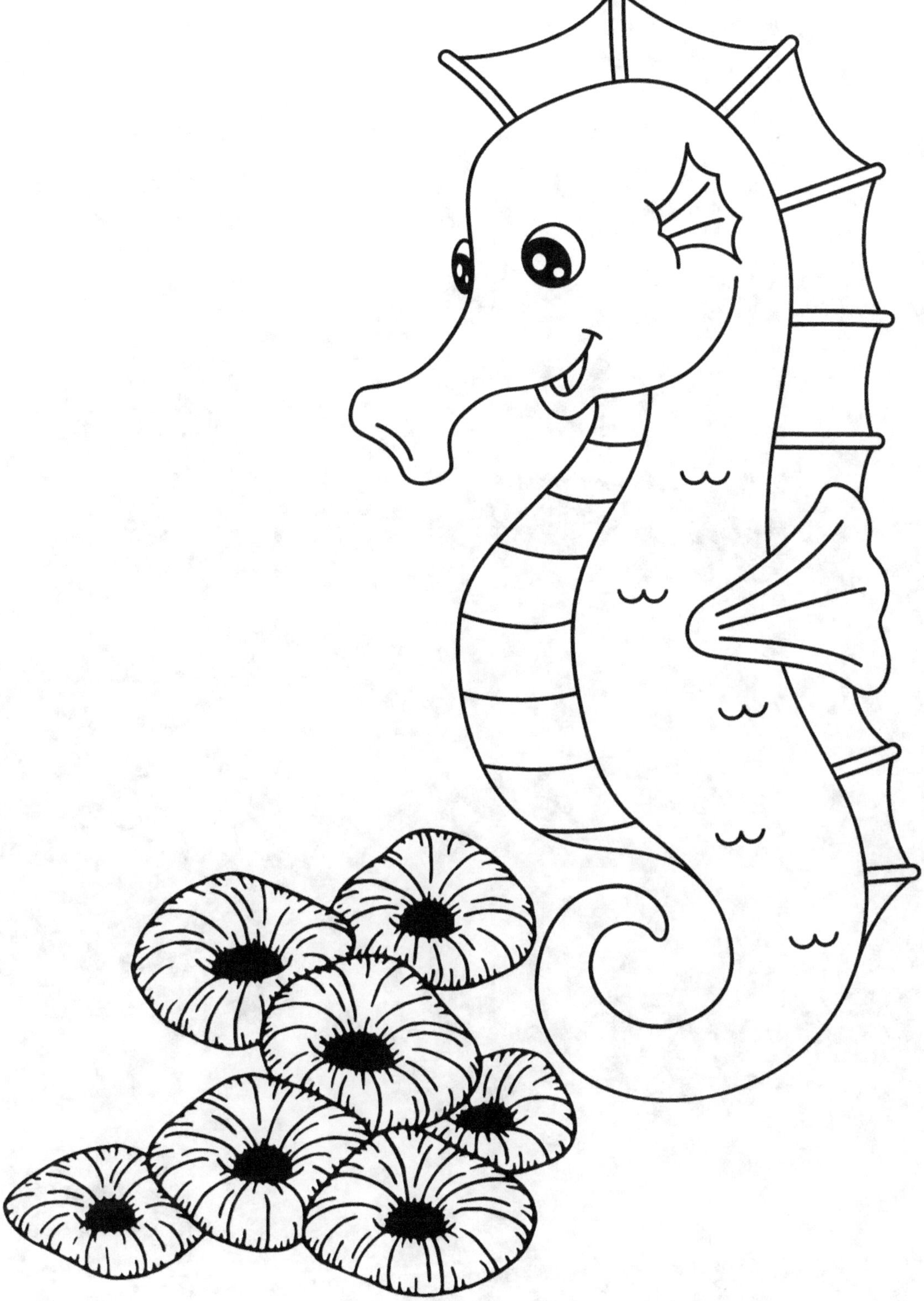

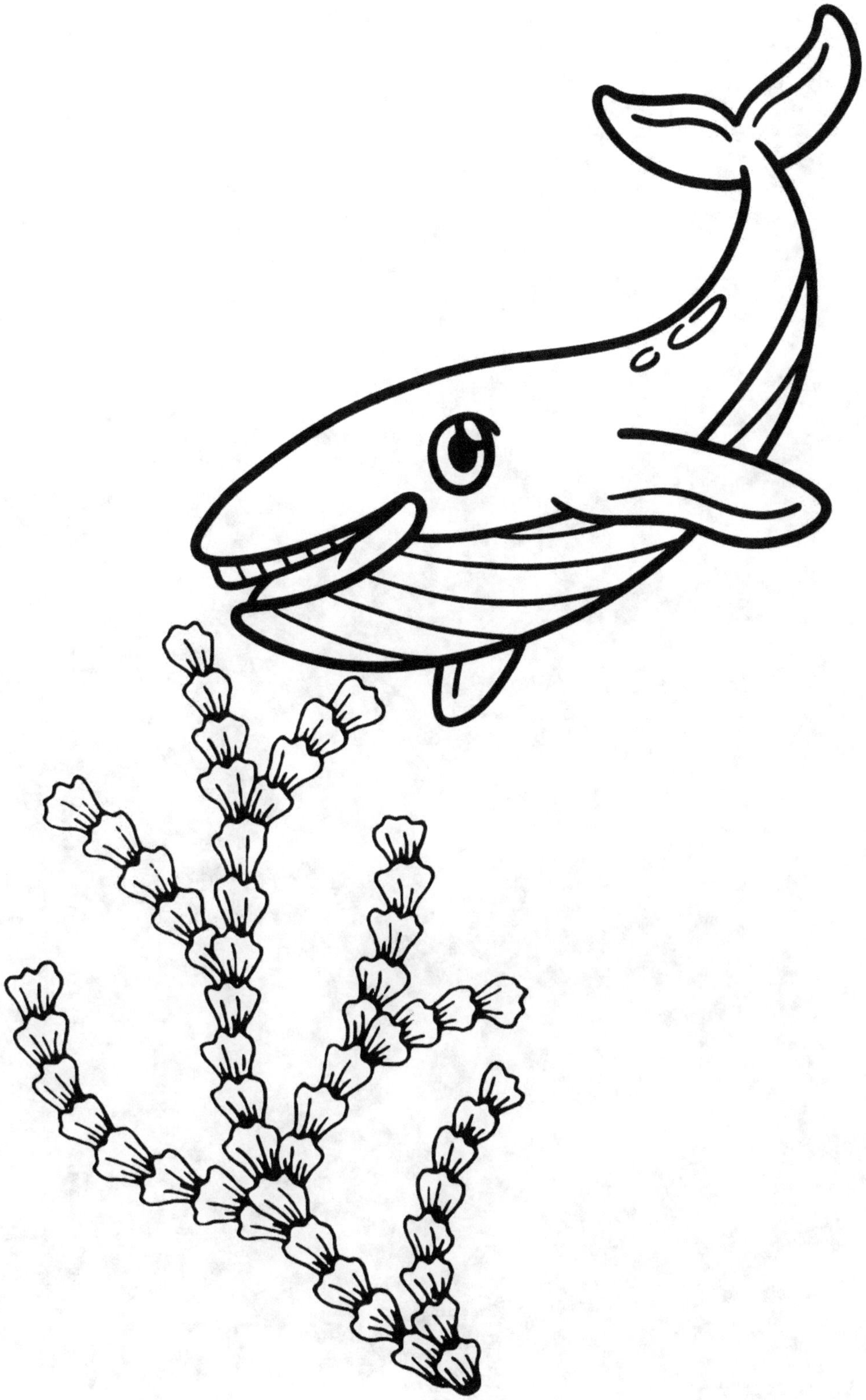

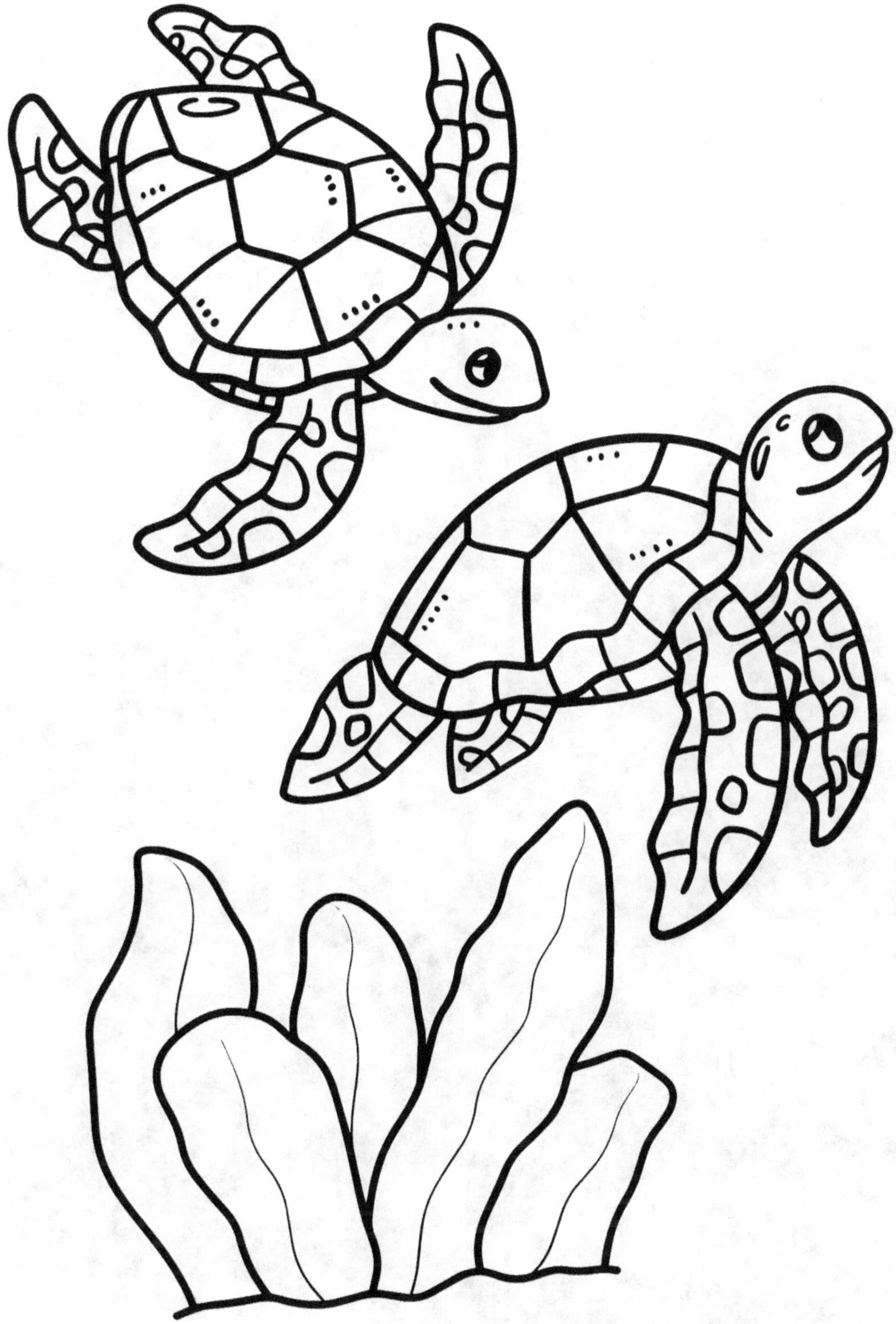

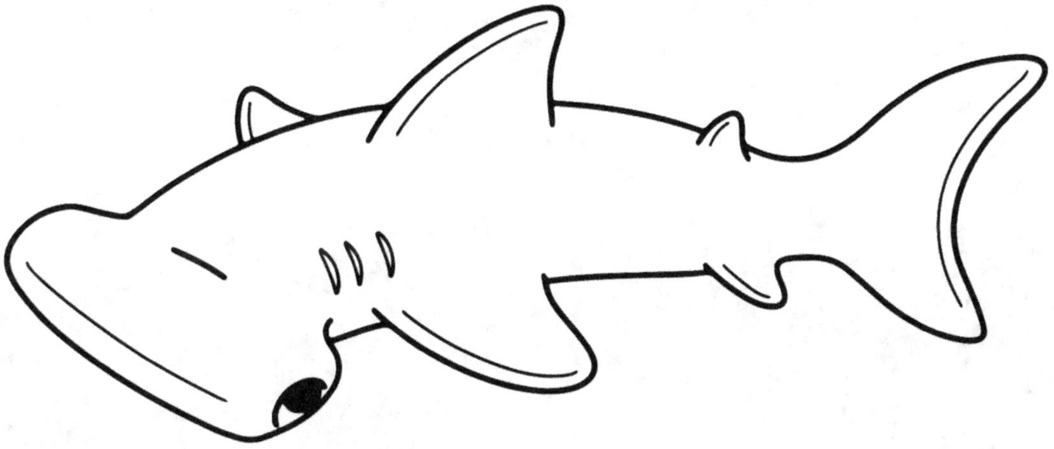
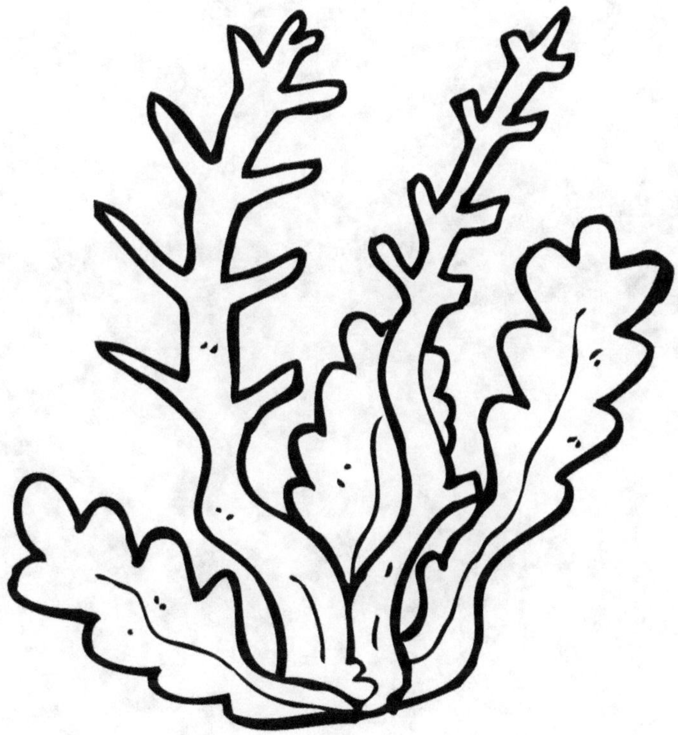

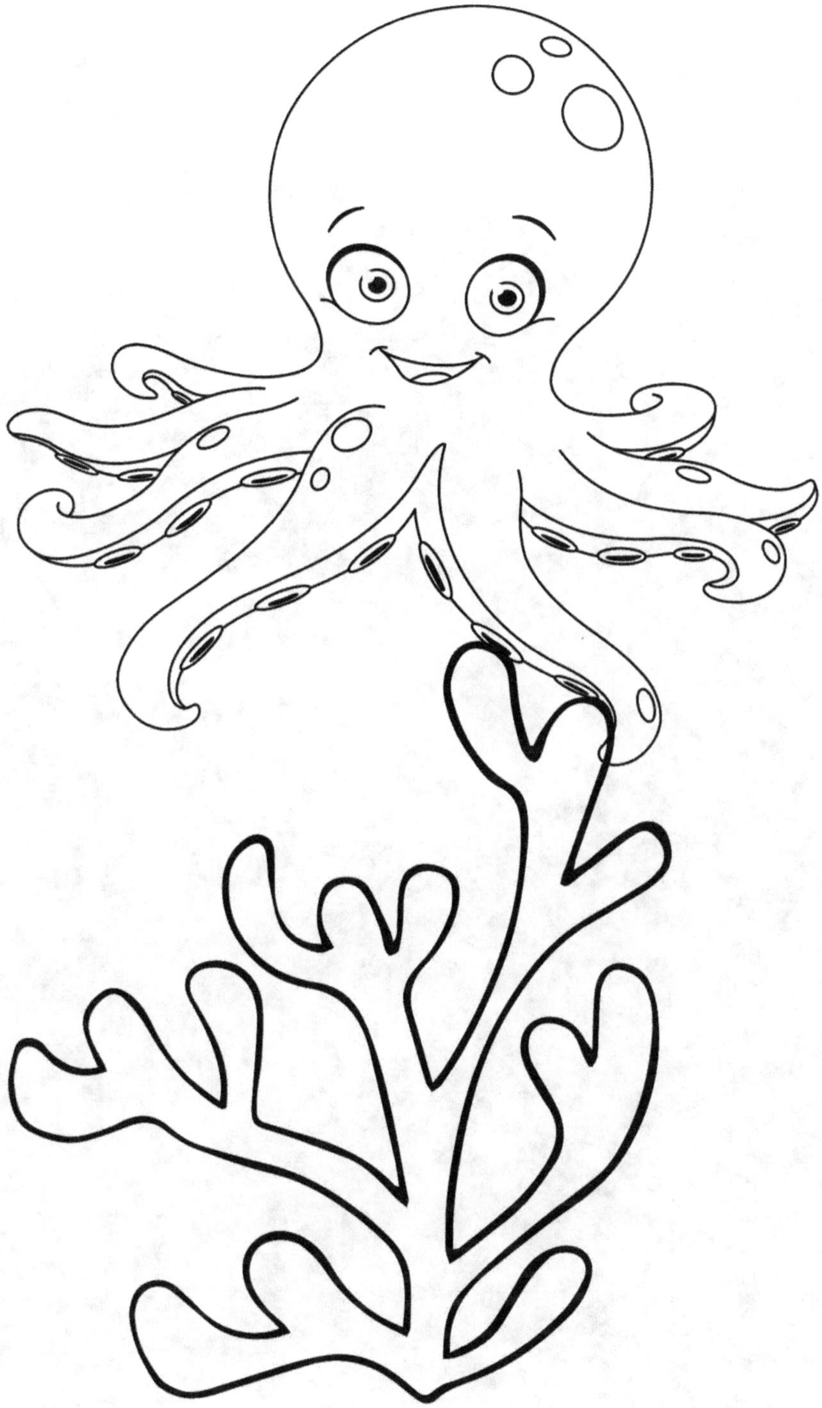

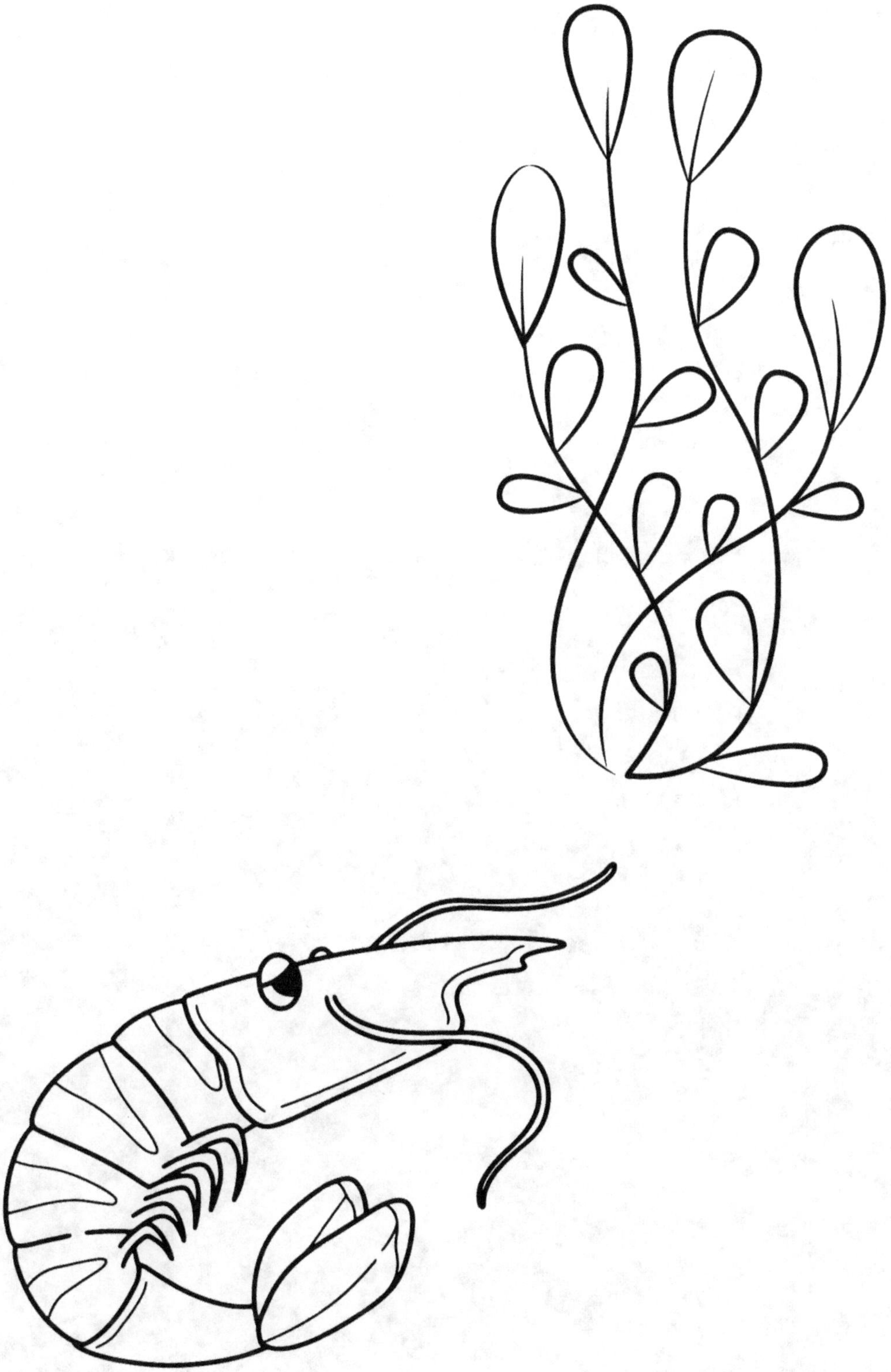

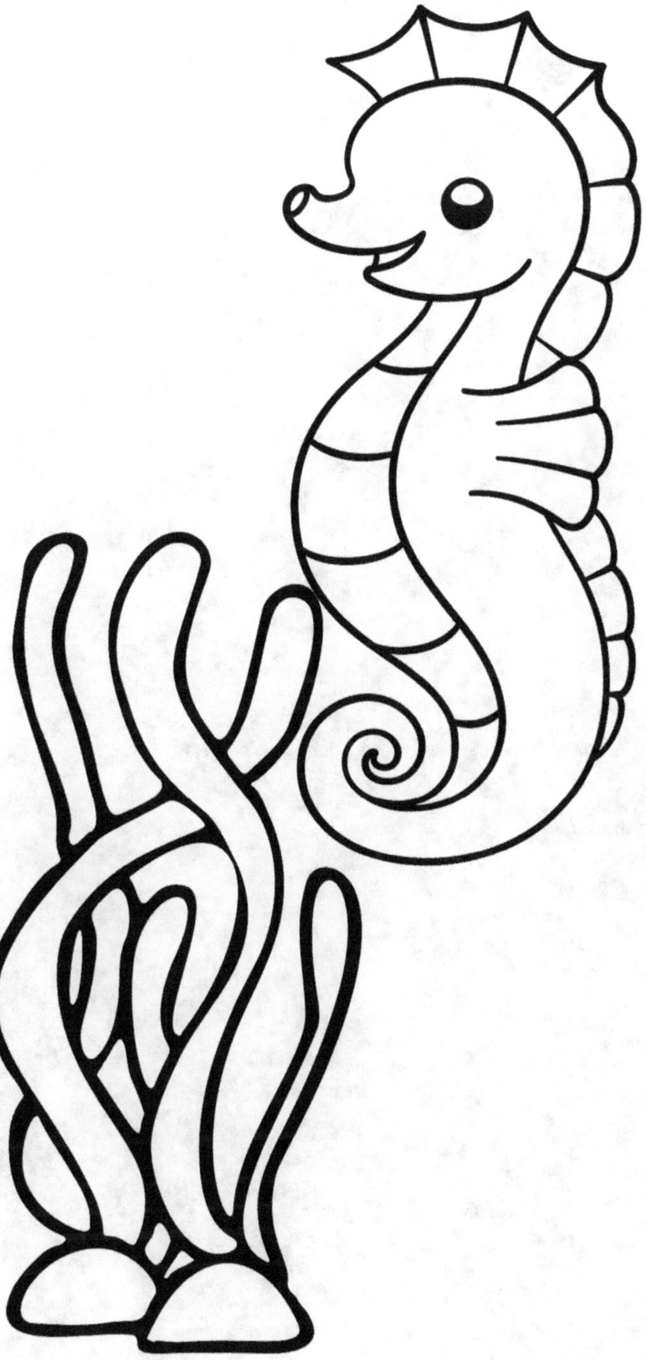

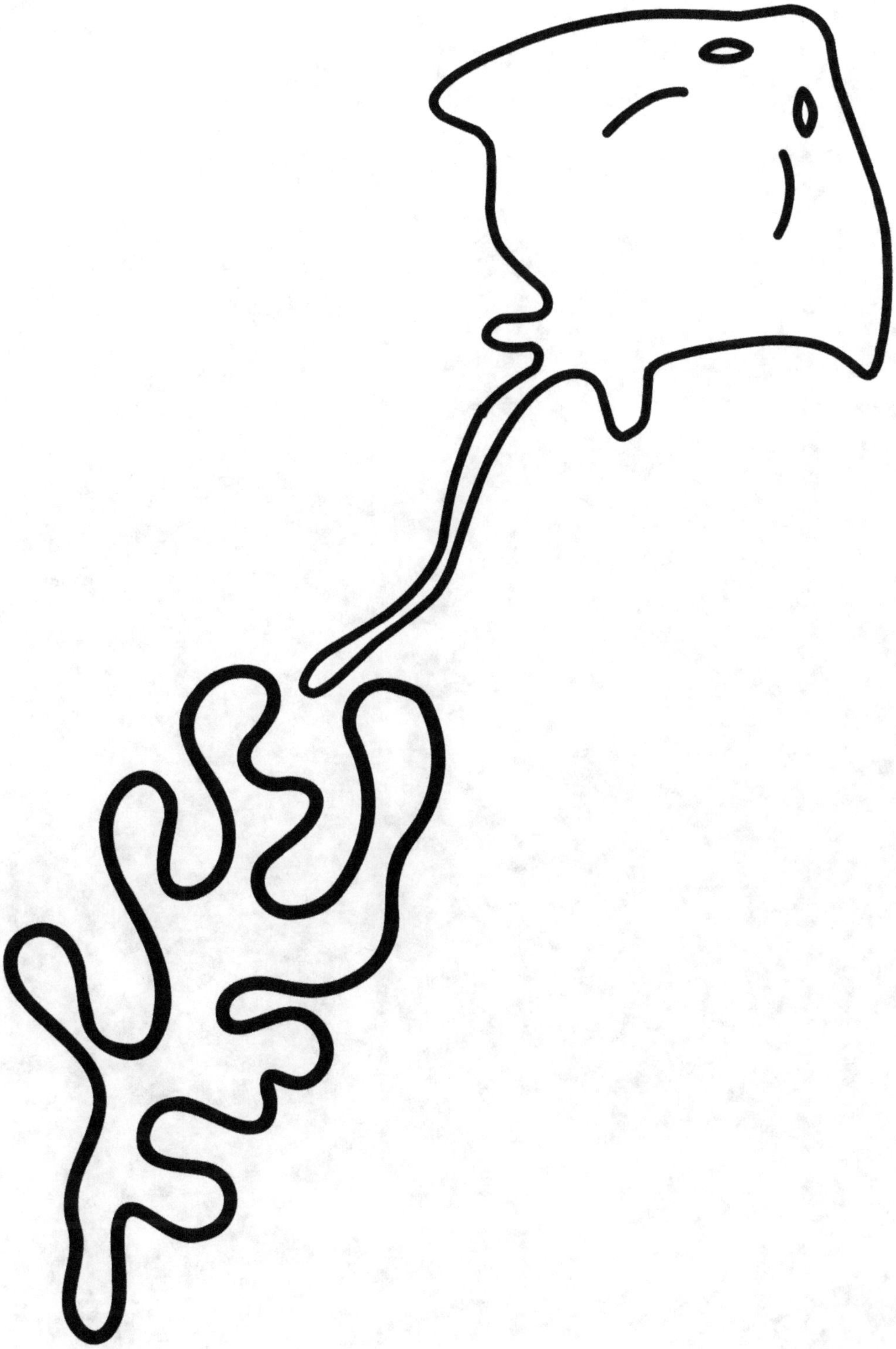

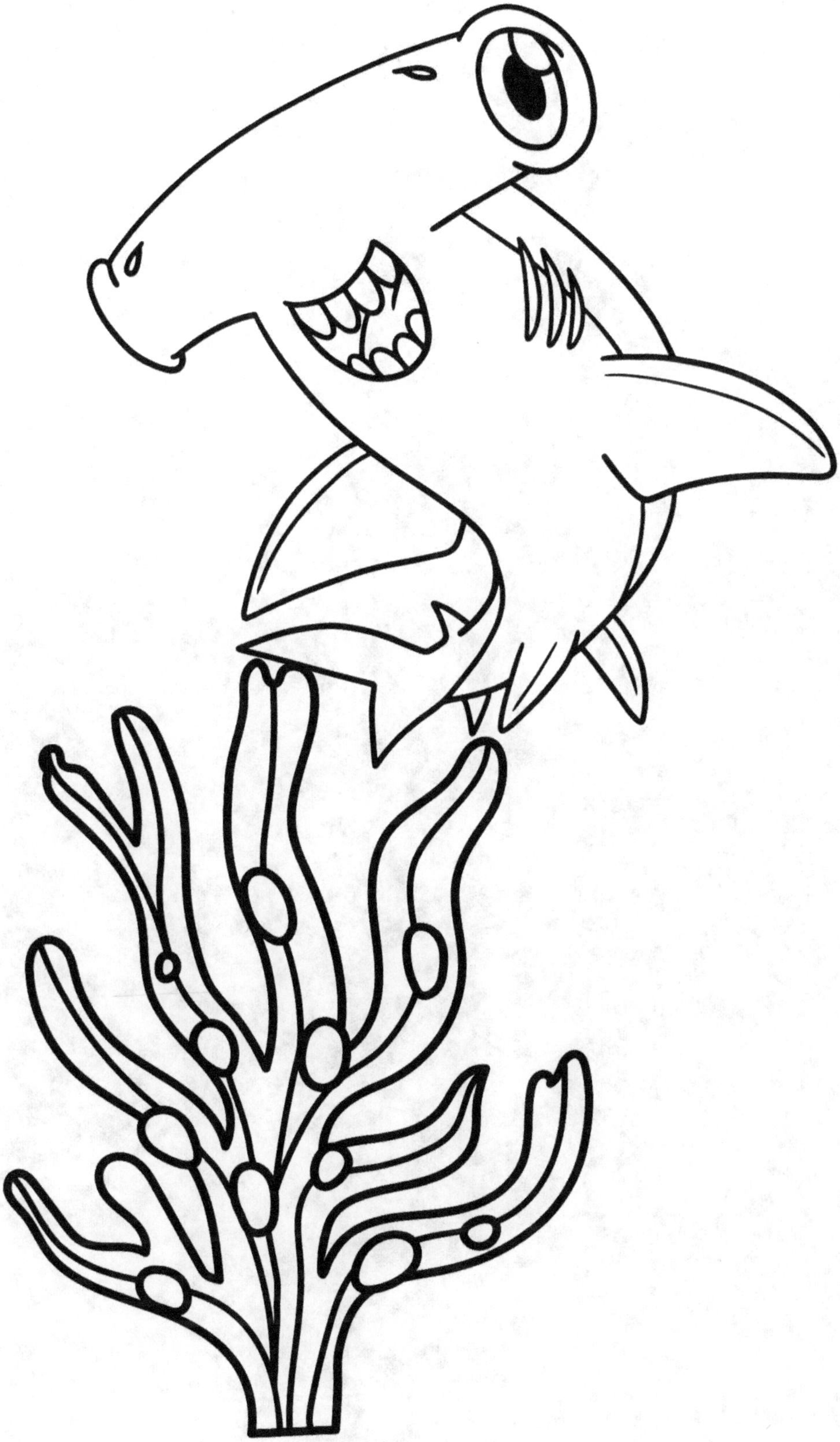

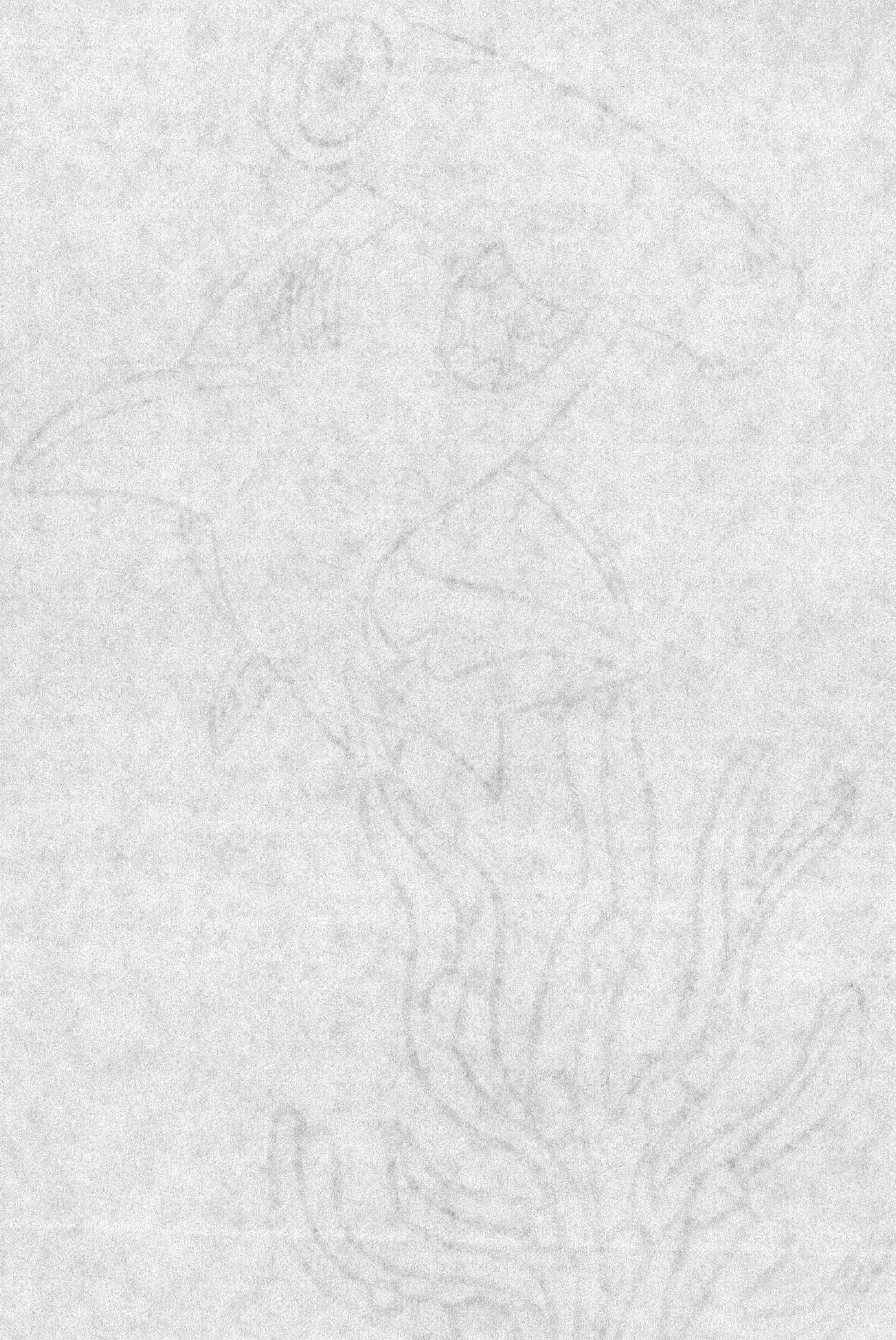

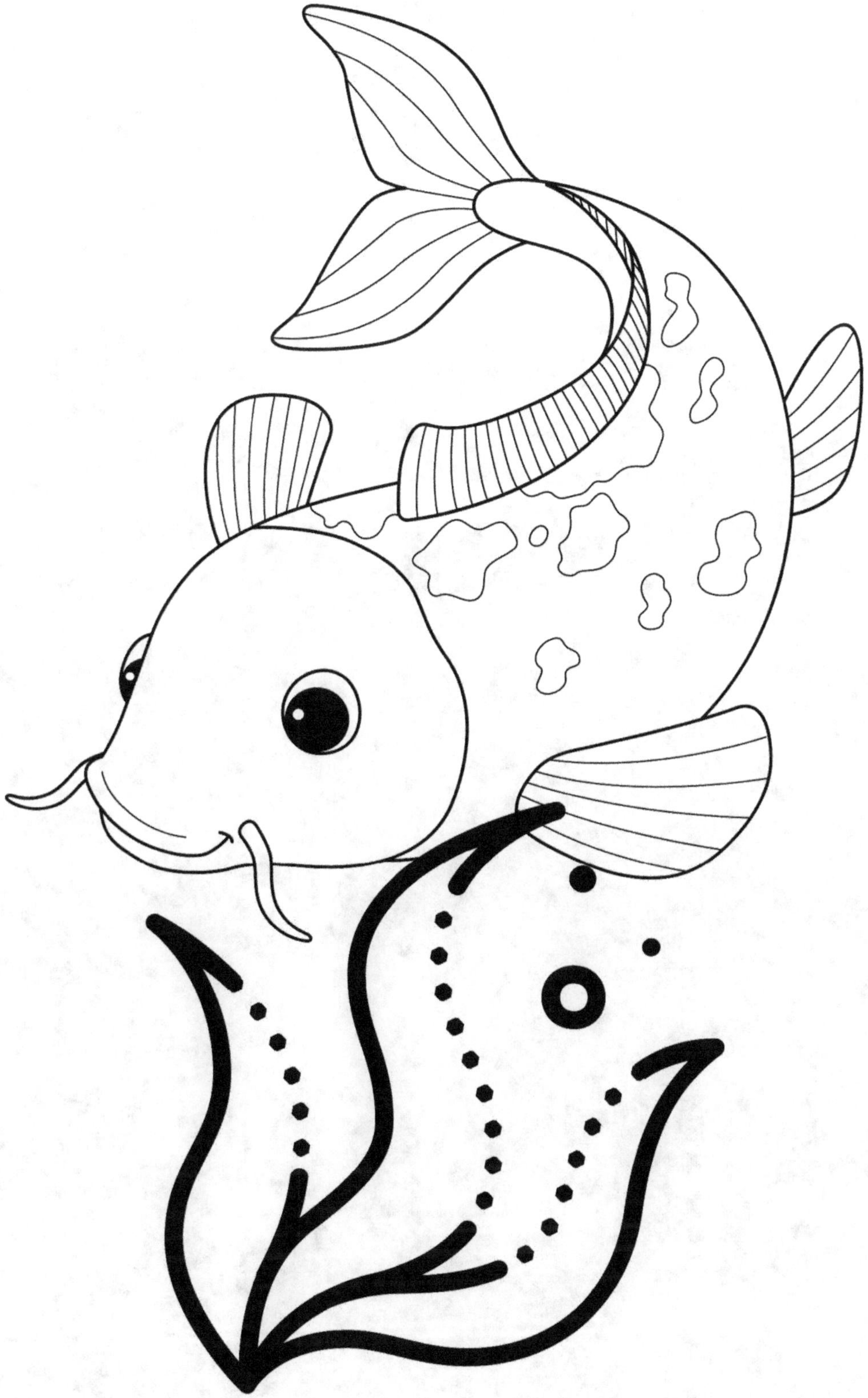

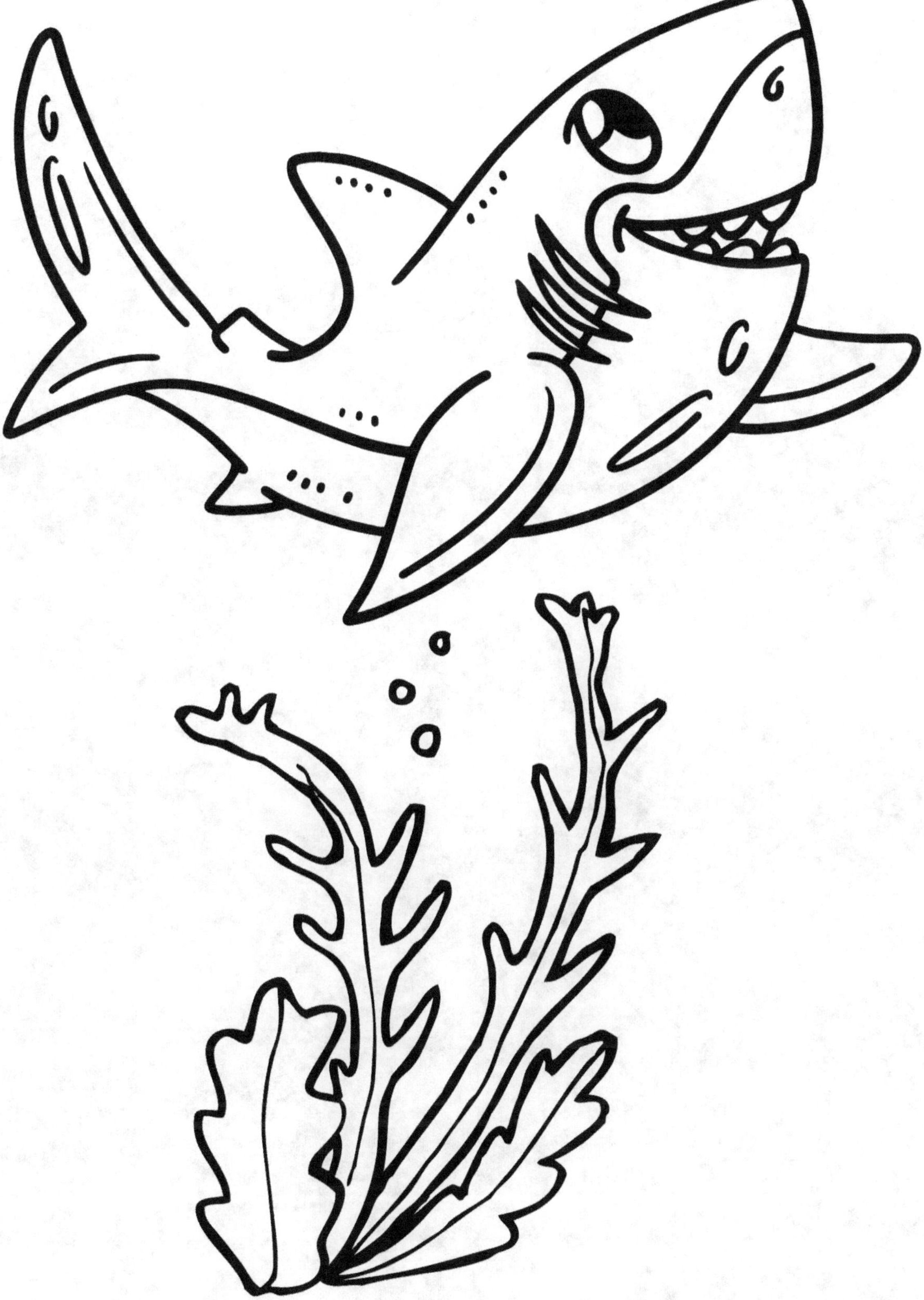

www.ingramcontent.com/pod-product-compliance
Lightning Source LLC
Chambersburg PA
CBHW081705220526
45466CB00009B/2884
9798396071612